Cotswolds Travel Guide 2023

Tour Guide to Discover Best things to do, Insider Tips, Must-See Attractions, and Idyllic Beautiful Villages in the Countryside

Charles J. Norris

Table of Contents

Introduction

Grateful have I been since I discovered a hidden gem nestled amidst the captivating landscapes of the English countryside—a place of undeniable beauty and captivating allure. This place, my dear fellow travelers, is none other than the enchanting Cotswolds.

As I set foot in this picturesque region for the first time, I was instantly spellbound by its timeless charm. The Cotswolds unfolded before me like a living painting, with its rolling hills dressed in velvety green, meandering rivers reflecting the azure sky, and villages that seemed plucked from the pages of a storybook. It was as if I had stumbled upon a secret realm, where tranquility and beauty reign supreme.

In the Cotswolds, time slows down, inviting you to pause, breathe, and immerse yourself in the wonders of the present moment. The hustle and bustle of everyday life fades into the background, replaced by a sense of serenity that seeps into your very being. It is a place where you can truly escape the chaos of the world and find solace in the gentle rhythm of nature.

With each passing day, I discovered the true essence of the Cotswolds—a place that effortlessly blends history, culture, and natural splendor. From the picturesque villages that dot the countryside to the awe-inspiring stately homes and castles that whisper tales of a bygone era, the Cotswolds offers a treasure trove of stories waiting to be unraveled.

But it is not only the tangible beauty that makes the Cotswolds a destination unlike any other. It is the intangible magic that lingers in the air—the warmth of the locals, the sense of community, and the genuine connection to the land. Whether sipping tea in a cozy tearoom, strolling through vibrant local markets, or engaging in lively conversations with passionate artisans, the Cotswolds embraces you as one of its own.

Now, dear traveler, imagine embarking on your own journey through the Cotswolds. Picture yourself exploring the charming villages, where time stands still and each corner reveals a new delight. Feel the thrill of wandering along ancient footpaths, breathing in the fresh scent of wildflowers, and witnessing the ever-changing colors of the seasons.

Immerse yourself in the rich tapestry of history, as you step inside grand stately homes that have witnessed centuries of stories unfold. Marvel at the architectural wonders of medieval churches and abbeys, their walls echoing with whispers of the past. Indulge your senses in the local cuisine, savoring the flavors of farm-fresh ingredients and traditional delicacies that have been passed down through generations.

But the Cotswolds offers more than just visual and culinary delights. It is a place where you can reconnect with nature, embrace the simple pleasures of life, and forge memories that will last a lifetime. Whether hiking along the renowned Cotswolds Way, cycling through breathtaking landscapes, or simply finding solace in the embrace of nature, this region invites you to awaken your adventurous spirit.

As you embark on this remarkable journey through the Cotswolds, let our comprehensive "Cotswolds Travel Guide" be your trusted companion. Within these pages, you will discover the hidden gems, must-see attractions, insider tips, and immersive experiences that will make your visit truly unforgettable. Let us be your guide as you navigate this magical realm, unlocking its secrets and immersing yourself in its undeniable allure.

So, fellow wanderer, are you ready to embark on an extraordinary adventure? Are you ready to lose yourself in the timeless beauty of the Cotswolds? Then join us on this remarkable journey, for the Cotswolds awaits, ready to captivate your heart and leave an indelible mark on your soul. Let us begin, together, and uncover the wonders of this enchanting region.

1. Welcome to the Cotswolds

Welcome to the Cotswolds, a region that beckons with its timeless beauty and captivating allure. In this introductory chapter, we will provide you with an overview of this enchanting region, delving into its unique characteristics and exploring why it is a destination that should be at the top of your travel list.

1.1 Overview of the Cotswolds Region

- Geographical Location: Discover the geographical boundaries of the Cotswolds, spanning across multiple counties in south-central England, and get a sense of its expansive beauty.

- Natural Landscapes: Explore the diverse landscapes that define the Cotswolds, from rolling hills and lush valleys to winding rivers and charming meadows. Gain an understanding of the region's natural wonders and the importance of conservation efforts.

- Historical Significance: Uncover the rich history of the Cotswolds, from its ancient roots as a center of the wool trade to its influence on English architecture and craftsmanship. Learn about the fascinating heritage that has shaped the region's identity.

- Cultural Tapestry: Dive into the vibrant cultural scene of the Cotswolds, which boasts a thriving arts and crafts community, lively festivals, and a deep connection to traditional customs and celebrations. Discover the artistic, literary, and musical contributions that have emerged from this creative hub.

1.2 Why Visit the Cotswolds

- Timeless Beauty: Delve into the captivating allure of the Cotswolds, where every village exudes charm and tranquility. Experience the region's idyllic landscapes, honey-colored limestone cottages, and quintessential English gardens that create a picturesque setting unlike any other.

- Architectural Marvels: Marvel at the architectural wonders that adorn the Cotswolds, including magnificent stately homes, historic churches, and medieval castles. Learn about the distinctive Cotswold stone used in construction and how it contributes to the region's architectural charm.

- Outdoor Adventures: Embark on thrilling outdoor adventures in the Cotswolds, with an array of activities to suit every interest. From scenic hikes along the Cotswold Way to cycling routes that showcase breathtaking vistas, the region offers endless opportunities for exploration and discovery.

- Culinary Delights: Indulge your taste buds in the Cotswolds' culinary delights, as you savor locally sourced ingredients and traditional dishes. From charming tearooms and cozy pubs to fine dining establishments, the Cotswolds offers a gastronomic journey that will delight food enthusiasts.

- Cultural Experiences: Immerse yourself in the Cotswolds' cultural tapestry through visits to museums, galleries, and workshops that showcase local arts, crafts, and traditions. Engage with the friendly locals and partake in the region's lively festivals and events, gaining insights into its vibrant community spirit.

- Relaxation and Wellness: Escape the hustle and bustle of everyday life as you immerse yourself in the Cotswolds' serene atmosphere. Experience moments of tranquility in scenic gardens, indulge in spa retreats, and find inner peace through yoga and meditation practices offered in the region.

- Authentic Village Life: Step into the Cotswolds' charming villages and discover the warmth and hospitality of the locals. Engage in friendly conversations, explore quaint shops and markets, and soak up the timeless ambiance that pervades these idyllic settings.

As you embark on your Cotswolds journey, let this guide be your trusted companion, providing you with insights, recommendations, and inspiration to make the most of your visit. Get ready to immerse yourself in the wonders of the Cotswolds and create memories that will last a lifetime.

Chapter 1: Planning Your Trip

1.1 Best Time to Visit the Cotswolds

The best time to visit the Cotswolds is during the spring or fall, when the weather is mild and the countryside is in bloom.

Spring (March-May)

The spring is a great time to visit the Cotswolds, as the weather is starting to warm up and the flowers are in bloom. This is a popular time for tourists, so be sure to book your accommodations early.

Summer (June-August)

The summer is the warmest time of year in the Cotswolds, and it is also the most crowded. The weather is usually sunny and dry, and there are plenty of activities to enjoy, such as hiking, biking, and swimming.

Fall (September-November)

The fall is a beautiful time to visit the Cotswolds, as the leaves change color and the weather is still mild. This is a less crowded time of year, so you can enjoy the scenery without the crowds.

Winter (December-February)

The winter can be cold and wet in the Cotswolds, but there are still plenty of things to do, such as visiting Christmas markets, going for walks in the snow, and enjoying the cozy atmosphere of the pubs.

1.2 Duration of Stay

The amount of time you need to spend in the Cotswolds will depend on what you want to do and see. If you are planning on doing some hiking or biking, you will need more time than if you are just planning on visiting the villages and towns.

A short trip to the Cotswolds can be as short as a weekend, but a longer trip of 3-4 days would be ideal. This would give you enough time to see the most popular attractions, such as Bibury, Bourton-on-the-Water, and Stow-on-the-Wold.

If you have more time, you could also explore some of the less-visited villages, such as Painswick, Broadway, and Chipping Campden. You could also go for a walk on the Cotswold Way, a 100-mile long-distance footpath that runs through the heart of the Cotswolds.

1.3 Getting to the Cotswolds

There are many ways to get to the Cotswolds, depending on your preferences and budget.

1.3.1 By Air

The nearest airports to the Cotswolds are Bristol Airport and Birmingham Airport. From either airport, you can take a train or bus to the Cotswolds.

Bristol Airport: Bristol Airport is located about 40 miles from the Cotswolds. There are several train services that run from Bristol Airport to the Cotswolds, including First Great Western and CrossCountry. The journey time is around 1 hour. There are also several bus services that run from Bristol Airport to the Cotswolds, including National Express and First Bus. The journey time is around 1.5 hours.

Birmingham Airport: Birmingham Airport is located about 60 miles from the Cotswolds. There are several train services that run from Birmingham Airport to the Cotswolds, including West Midlands Railway and CrossCountry. The journey time is around 1 hour 30 minutes. There are also several bus services that run from Birmingham Airport to the Cotswolds, including National Express and First Bus. The journey time is around 2 hours.

1.3.2 By Train

The Cotswolds is well-served by train services. There are several train stations in the Cotswolds, including Cheltenham Spa, Stroud, and Moreton-in-Marsh. From any of these stations, you can easily reach the other villages and towns in the Cotswolds.

Cheltenham Spa: Cheltenham Spa is a popular tourist destination in the Cotswolds. The town is home to a number of attractions, including the Cheltenham Racecourse, the Cheltenham Spa Pump Room, and the Cheltenham Art Gallery and Museum.

Stroud: Stroud is a town in the Cotswolds that is known for its arts and crafts scene. The town is home to a number of galleries, studios, and shops.

Moreton-in-Marsh: Moreton-in-Marsh is a market town in the Cotswolds that is a popular base for exploring the region. The town is home to a number of shops, restaurants, and pubs.

1.3.3 By Car

The Cotswolds is also easily accessible by car. There are several major roads that run through the Cotswolds, including the M40, the M5, and the A46. If you are driving to the Cotswolds, be sure to allow plenty of time for traffic, especially during peak tourist season.

Tips for Getting to the Cotswolds

Book your flights or train tickets in advance, especially if you are traveling during peak tourist season.

If you are traveling by car, be sure to fill up your tank before you leave.

Allow plenty of time for traffic, especially if you are traveling during peak tourist season.

Consider renting a car if you want to explore the Cotswolds at your own pace.

There are several car rental companies that have offices in the Cotswolds.

Be sure to bring your camera.

The Cotswolds is a beautiful region and you will want to capture your memories on film.

1.4 Navigating the Cotswolds

There are many ways to get around the Cotswolds, depending on your budget and preferences.

Public Transportation

The Cotswolds is well-served by public transportation, making it easy to get around without a car. The main operator is First Great Western, which operates trains between London and Oxford, as well as local services to other towns in the Cotswolds. There are also a number of bus services, which can be a more scenic way to travel.

If you're planning on doing a lot of exploring, you may want to consider getting a Cotswolds Discovery

Pass. This pass gives you unlimited travel on First Great Western trains and buses in the Cotswolds for a set period of time.

Renting a Car

If you want to have more flexibility and explore the Cotswolds at your own pace, you may want to consider renting a car. There are a number of car rental companies operating in the Cotswolds, so you should be able to find one that fits your budget.

When renting a car, be sure to factor in the cost of fuel, parking, and insurance. You may also want to consider getting a GPS device, as some of the roads in the Cotswolds can be a bit tricky to navigate.

Driving in the Cotswolds

Driving in the Cotswolds can be a bit challenging, as the roads are narrow and winding. There are also a number of villages with narrow streets and one-way systems. Be sure to be patient and drive slowly, especially when there are other cars around.

Parking can also be a challenge, especially in the more popular towns and villages. If possible, try to park in a car park and walk to your destination.

Tips for Navigating the Cotswolds

Plan your route in advance. This will help you avoid getting lost, especially if you're not familiar with the area.

Use a map or GPS device. This will help you stay on track and make sure you don't miss any of the sights.

Be patient. The Cotswolds is a popular tourist destination, so expect traffic to be heavy at times.

Enjoy the scenery! The Cotswolds is a beautiful region, so take some time to relax and enjoy the view.

1.5 Accommodation Options

There are many different accommodation options available to suit all budgets and tastes. Here are a few suggestions:

Bed and breakfasts (B&Bs) are a great way to experience the Cotswolds at a more affordable price. Many B&Bs are located in charming cottages or converted farmhouses, and they often offer home-cooked breakfasts and evening meals.

Inns are another popular option for accommodation in the Cotswolds. Inns are typically larger than B&Bs, and they often have bars and restaurants. Some inns have been in business for centuries, and they offer a unique glimpse into the history of the Cotswolds.

Country houses are a luxurious option for accommodation in the Cotswolds. Many country houses have been converted into hotels, and they offer a variety of amenities, such as swimming pools, tennis courts, and golf courses.

Self-catering cottages are a great option for families or groups of friends. Cottages come in all shapes and sizes, and they can be found in both rural and urban areas. Many cottages have their own gardens, and some even have hot tubs or saunas.

When choosing accommodation in the Cotswolds, it is important to consider your budget, your needs, and your interests. If you are looking for a romantic getaway, a country house hotel may be the perfect option for you. If you are traveling with children, a self-catering cottage may be a better choice. And if you are on a tight budget, a B&B or inn may be the best option.

No matter what your budget or needs, you are sure to find the perfect accommodation in the Cotswolds.

Here are some additional tips for choosing accommodation in the Cotswolds:

Book your accommodation in advance, especially if you are traveling during peak season (June-August).

Consider the location of your accommodation. If you want to be close to the major tourist attractions, choose a hotel or B&B in a town or village. If you prefer a more rural setting, choose a country house or self-catering cottage.

Read reviews of different accommodation options before you book. This will help you to get an idea of the quality of the accommodation and the level of service that you can expect.

Ask about discounts and special offers. Many hotels, B&Bs, and inns offer discounts for longer stays or for booking in advance.

Chapter 2: Exploring the Countryside

2.1 Charming Villages of the Cotswolds

2.1.1 Bourton-on-the-Water

Bourton-on-the-Water is a charming village in the Cotswolds, England. It is known for its beautiful stone cottages, its riverside location, and its many attractions, including the Cotswold Motoring Museum, Birdland, and the Model Village.

History

Bourton-on-the-Water has been inhabited for centuries. The first evidence of human settlement in the area dates back to the Iron Age. The village was later founded by the Romans, who built a settlement on the banks of the River Windrush. In the Middle Ages, Bourton-on-the-Water was an important market town. It was also a popular destination for pilgrims, who visited the village to see the shrine of St. Mary.

Attractions

Bourton-on-the-Water is home to a number of attractions, including:

The Cotswold Motoring Museum: This museum houses a collection of vintage cars, motorcycles, and toy cars.

Birdland: This wildlife park is home to over 500 birds from around the world.

The Model Village: This miniature village is a replica of Bourton-on-the-Water, complete with its bridges, houses, and shops.

The Bourton-on-the-Water Museum: This museum tells the story of the village's history.

The Cotswold Water Park: This water park is located just outside of Bourton-on-the-Water. It offers a variety of water activities, including swimming, boating, and fishing.

Things to do

In addition to visiting the attractions listed above, there are many other things to do in Bourton-on-the-Water. Here are a few suggestions:

Take a stroll along the River Windrush: The River Windrush runs through the center of Bourton-on-the-Water. It is a great place to take a stroll, admire the scenery, and spot some wildlife.

Visit the Bourton-on-the-Water shops: Bourton-on-the-Water has a number of charming shops, selling everything from souvenirs to antiques.

Enjoy a meal at one of the village's restaurants: Bourton-on-the-Water has a number of excellent restaurants, serving everything from traditional English fare to international cuisine.

Have a drink at one of the village's pubs: Bourton-on-the-Water has a number of traditional pubs, where you can enjoy a pint of local ale and soak up the atmosphere.

Take a boat trip on the River Windrush: There are a number of companies that offer boat trips on the River Windrush. This is a great way to see the village from a different perspective and get up close to the wildlife.

Go for a hike or bike ride in the surrounding countryside: The Cotswolds are a beautiful area of countryside. There are a number of hiking and biking trails in the area, which offer stunning views of the countryside.

Getting there

Bourton-on-the-Water is located in the Cotswolds, England. It is about 100 miles (160 kilometers) northwest of London. The nearest train station is Bourton-on-the-Water railway station. There are also a number of bus services that stop in Bourton-on-the-Water.

Accommodation

There are a number of hotels, bed and breakfasts, and self-catering accommodation in Bourton-on-the-Water.

Tips

The best time to visit Bourton-on-the-Water is during the spring or fall, when the weather is mild and the crowds are smaller.

If you are planning to visit Bourton-on-the-Water during the summer, be sure to book your accommodation and activities in advance.

Bourton-on-the-Water can be a very popular tourist destination, so be prepared for crowds, especially on weekends and during the summer holidays.

2.1.2 Stow-on-the-Wold

Stow-on-the-Wold is a charming Cotswold village with a rich history and a thriving community. It is located in the heart of the Cotswolds, an Area of Outstanding Natural Beauty, and is a popular destination for visitors from all over the world.

Stow-on-the-Wold was founded in the 11th century and grew in importance as a market town during the

Middle Ages. It was a major stop on the Cotswold Way, an ancient route that linked London with Bristol. The village was also a center for the wool trade, and its many weavers and clothiers helped to make Stow-on-the-Wold a prosperous town.

Today, Stow-on-the-Wold is a popular tourist destination, known for its beautiful architecture, its charming shops and restaurants, and its many events and attractions. The village is also a popular destination for walkers and cyclists, who can explore the surrounding countryside on a variety of trails.

Here are some of the things you can do in Stow-on-the-Wold:

Visit the Stow-on-the-Wold Museum: This museum tells the story of the village's history, from its founding to the present day.
Take a stroll along the High Street: The High Street is the main street in Stow-on-the-Wold, and it is lined with charming shops, restaurants, and pubs.

Visit the Cotswold Perfumery: This perfumery offers a variety of tours and workshops, where you can learn about the art of perfume making.

Go for a walk or bike ride in the surrounding countryside: The Cotswolds are a beautiful area of countryside, and there are a number of trails that you can explore.

Visit the Stow-on-the-Wold Farmers Market: This market is held every Saturday morning, and it is a great place to buy fresh produce, meats, and cheeses.

Attend one of the village's many events: Stow-on-the-Wold hosts a number of events throughout the year, including the Cotswolds International Music Festival, the Stow-on-the-Wold Food Festival, and the Stow-on-the-Wold Christmas Fayre.

If you are looking for a charming and historic village to visit in the Cotswolds, Stow-on-the-Wold is a great option. With its beautiful architecture, its thriving community, and its many attractions, Stow-on-the-Wold is sure to charm you.

2.1.3 Bibury

Bibury is a small village in the Cotswolds, England. It is known for its beautiful honey-colored stone cottages, which are reflected in the River Coln that runs through the village. Bibury was originally a Saxon settlement, and it was mentioned in the Domesday Book in 1086. The village grew in importance during the Middle Ages, as it was a major center for the wool trade. Bibury is a popular tourist destination, and it is often described as one of the most beautiful villages in England. The village is a popular spot for photographers, and it has been featured in many films and television shows. Some of the things you can do in Bibury include:

Visit the Arlington Row: This row of weavers' cottages is one of the most photographed spots in Bibury.

Take a walk along the River Coln: This is a great way to see the village from a different perspective and spot some wildlife.

Visit the Bibury Trout Farm: This farm offers fishing for trout, as well as a restaurant and gift shop.

Visit the Bibury Parish Church: This church was built in the 12th century, and it is a Grade I listed building.

If you are looking for a charming and picturesque village to visit in the Cotswolds, Bibury is a great option. With its beautiful architecture, its tranquil setting, and its many attractions, Bibury is sure to charm you.

2.1.4 Broadway

Broadway is a charming village in the Cotswolds, England. It is located in the county of Worcestershire, about two hours from London. The village is known for its beautiful architecture, its wide main street, and its many shops and restaurants.

Broadway was originally a small hamlet, but it grew in size and importance in the 16th and 17th centuries. During this time, the village was a popular stop for stagecoaches traveling between London and Oxford. Broadway also became a center for the wool trade, and many wealthy merchants built large houses in the village.

Today, Broadway is a popular tourist destination. Visitors come to enjoy the village's historic architecture, its scenic setting, and its many attractions. Some of the most popular attractions in Broadway include:

The Lygon Arms: This historic hotel has been in operation since the 14th century. It is a popular spot for both tourists and locals.

Broadway Tower: This tower was built in the 18th century. It offers stunning views of the surrounding countryside.

The Cotswold Perfumery: This perfumery has been in operation since the 1970s. It offers a variety of unique fragrances made from natural ingredients.

Broadway Arts Festival: This festival is held every year in July. It features a variety of art exhibitions, concerts, and theater performances.

In addition to its many attractions, Broadway is also a great place to simply relax and enjoy the scenery. The village is surrounded by rolling hills and lush countryside. There are plenty of opportunities for hiking, biking, and horseback riding.

If you are looking for a charming and picturesque village to visit in the Cotswolds, Broadway is a great option. The village has something to offer everyone, from history buffs to nature lovers to shopaholics.

Here are some other things to do in Broadway:

Visit the Broadway Museum: This museum tells the story of Broadway's history and its role in the wool trade.
Take a walk along the Broadway Walk: This scenic walk takes you past some of Broadway's most popular attractions, including the Lygon Arms, Broadway Tower, and the Cotswold Perfumery.

Enjoy a meal at one of Broadway's many restaurants: Broadway has a wide variety of restaurants to choose from, serving everything from traditional English fare to international cuisine.

Browse the shops in Broadway's High Street: Broadway's High Street is lined with charming shops selling everything from antiques to clothing to souvenirs.

Visit the Broadway Arts Centre: This theater hosts a variety of performances, including plays, musicals, and concerts.

Here are some tips for planning your trip to Broadway:

The best time to visit Broadway is during the spring or fall, when the weather is mild and the crowds are smaller.

Broadway is a popular tourist destination, so be sure to book your accommodations in advance.

There are a variety of ways to get to Broadway. You can drive, take a train, or take a bus.

Broadway is a small village, so you can easily get around on foot or by bike.

Broadway is a great place to relax and enjoy the scenery. Be sure to take some time to explore the village and its surroundings.

2.1.5 Castle Combe

Castle Combe is a beautiful village in the Cotswolds, England. It is known for its honey-colored stone cottages, its winding streets, and its picturesque market square. The village is small, with a population of just over 300 people, but it is a popular tourist destination.

Castle Combe was founded in the 12th century, and it grew up around a Norman castle. The castle was demolished in the 17th century, but the village still retains its medieval character. The village is a popular filming location, and it has appeared in films such as "Dr. Doolittle," "The Wolf Man," and "Stardust."

There are many things to see and do in Castle Combe. Visitors can wander the village's streets, admiring the architecture. They can also visit the market square, where there are several shops and cafes. The village also has a number of historical sites, including St. Andrew's Church, which dates back to the 13th century.

Castle Combe is a charming village that is perfect for a day trip. It is a great place to relax and enjoy the English countryside.

Here are some of the things you can do in Castle Combe:

Visit the market square: The market square is the heart of Castle Combe. It is a great place to wander around, admire the architecture, and do some shopping. There are several shops and cafes in the square, so you can also grab a bite to eat or do some souvenir shopping.

Visit St. Andrew's Church: St. Andrew's Church is a 13th-century church that is worth a visit. The church is free to enter, and it is a beautiful example of medieval architecture.

Take a walk through the village: The best way to experience Castle Combe is to simply wander through the village. The streets are lined with honey-colored cottages, and there are plenty of places to stop and take photos.

Go for a hike: There are several hiking trails in the area surrounding Castle Combe. These trails offer stunning views of the countryside, and they are a great way to get some exercise.

Have a picnic: The village has a number of parks and green spaces where you can have a picnic. This is a great way to enjoy the beautiful scenery and relax in the fresh air.

If you are looking for a charming and picturesque village to visit in the Cotswolds, then Castle Combe is a great option. It is a small village with a lot to offer visitors.

2.2 Cotswolds Way: A Scenic Hiking Trail

The Cotswolds Way is a 102-mile (164-kilometer) long-distance footpath in England that runs from Chipping Campden in Gloucestershire to Bath in Somerset. It is one of the most popular hiking trails in the UK, and for good reason. The Cotswolds are a beautiful area of rolling hills, lush meadows, and historic villages, and the Cotswolds Way offers stunning views of the surrounding countryside.

For hikers of all skill levels, the well-maintained and simple-to-follow track is a fantastic alternative. You may take your time and soak in the beauty because there are many spots to stop and rest along the road.

If you're looking for a challenging hike, the Cotswolds Way can be completed in four to five days. However, if you're short on time, you can also choose to hike shorter sections of the trail.

Here are some of the highlights of the Cotswolds Way:

Chipping Campden: This picturesque town is a great place to start your hike. It's full of medieval buildings, cobbled streets, and traditional Cotswolds architecture.

Broadway: This village is known for its stunning views of the surrounding countryside. It's also home to a number of pubs and restaurants, making it a great place to stop for lunch or dinner.

Stow-on-the-Wold: This market town is a great place to stock up on supplies before continuing your hike. It's also home to a number of historical buildings, including the Stow-on-the-Wold Town Hall and the St. Edward's Church.

Painswick: This village is known for its "pepperpot" cottages, which are small, round houses with distinctive roofs. It's also home to the Painswick Rococo Garden, a beautiful garden that was designed in the 18th century.

Bath: This UNESCO World Heritage city is a great place to end your hike. It's known for its Roman baths, Georgian architecture, and Jane Austen connections.

The Cotswolds Way is a great way to experience the beauty of the Cotswolds countryside. If you're looking for a challenging hike with stunning views, this is the trail for you.

Following are some ideas for organizing your hike:

The Cotswolds Way is best hiked in the spring or fall when the weather is nice and there are less hikers around.

Because there are few facilities along the trail, make sure you take plenty of water and snacks.

Don hiking-appropriate footwear, such as boots or shoes that are comfy.

Tell someone where you're going and when you anticipate returning.

Be aware of the weather forecast and be prepared for changes in the weather.

Enjoy the scenery and take your time!

2.3 Gardens and Parks

The area is also home to a number of stunning gardens and parks, which are popular attractions for visitors from all over the world.

Some of the most popular gardens in the Cotswolds include:

Barrington Court: This Elizabethan manor house is surrounded by beautiful gardens, which are open to the public from April to October. The gardens feature a variety of plants and flowers, as well as a number of interesting features, such as a maze, a sunken garden, and a water garden.

Hidcote Manor Garden: This Arts and Crafts garden is one of the most popular in the Cotswolds. The garden is known for its use of color, its variety of plants, and its interesting design features.

Kiftsgate Court Gardens: These gardens are located on a hillside and offer stunning views of the surrounding countryside. The gardens feature a variety of plants, including roses, rhododendrons, and azaleas.

Painswick Rococo Garden: This garden is a unique example of a Rococo garden, which is a style of garden that was popular in the 18th century. The garden features a number of interesting features, such as a grotto, a maze, and a sundial.

Sudeley Castle Gardens: These gardens are located around a medieval castle and feature a variety of plants, including roses, lavender, and herbs. The gardens also feature a number of interesting features, such as a maze, a water garden, and a sunken garden.

In addition to these popular gardens, there are many other beautiful gardens and parks in the Cotswolds. If you are planning a visit to the area, be sure to do some research and find the gardens that are most appealing to you.

2.4 Wildlife and Nature Reserves

Here are the best wildlife and nature reserves in the Cotswolds:

Cotswold Falconry Centre: This centre offers visitors the chance to see a variety of birds of prey up close, including hawks, owls, and falcons. There are also educational displays about the birds and their habitats.

Birdland: This zoo is home to over 500 birds from around the world. Visitors can see birds in their natural habitats, including rainforests, grasslands, and wetlands.

Westonbirt Arboretum: This arboretum is home to over 17,000 trees and shrubs from all over the world. There are also a number of gardens, lakes, and ponds.

Walks With Hawks: This company offers guided walks with trained hawks. Visitors can learn about the hawks and their behavior, and they may even get to hold a hawk.

WWT Slimbridge Wetland Centre: This wetland centre is home to over 2,500 birds from around the world. Visitors can see birds in their natural habitats, including marshes, meadows, and woodlands.

Cirencester Park: This park is home to a variety of wildlife, including deer, rabbits, and foxes. There are also a number of walking trails and a lake.

The Severn Ham: This nature reserve is home to a variety of wildlife, including waterfowl, waders, and mammals. There are also a number of walking trails and a visitor center.

Cotswold Alpacas: This farm is home to a herd of alpacas. Visitors can learn about alpacas and their fleece, and they may even get to feed and pet an alpaca.

The Barn Owl Centre: This centre is home to a number of barn owls. Visitors can learn about barn owls and their conservation, and they may even get to see a baby barn owl.

Greystones Farm: This farm is home to a variety of animals, including pigs, cows, and sheep. Visitors can learn about farming and see where their food comes from.

These are just a few of the many wildlife and nature reserves in the Cotswolds. With so much to see and do, you're sure to have a great time exploring this beautiful area.

Additional tips for planning your visit:

Dress in layers, as the weather can change quickly in the countryside.
Wear comfortable shoes, as you'll be doing a lot of walking.
Bring a camera, as you'll want to capture all the amazing wildlife you see.
Be respectful of the wildlife and their habitats.
Stay on the trails, as this helps to protect the environment.
Bring a picnic lunch, as there may not be any food available at the reserve.
Allow plenty of time to explore, as there is often a lot to see.

2.5 Cycling Routes

There are many great cycling routes to explore in the Cotswolds. Here are a few suggestions:

The Cotswold Way: This is a long-distance route that runs for 100 miles from Chipping Campden to Bath. It's a relatively easy ride, with some gentle hills and plenty of scenic countryside to enjoy.

The Broadway Tower Circular: This is a shorter route that starts and ends in Broadway, a charming Cotswold village. The ride is mostly flat, with some good views of the surrounding countryside.

The Bibury Circular: This is another short and easy route that takes in the picturesque village of Bibury, known for its honey-colored cottages and idyllic riverside setting.

The Cirencester Circular: This is a longer and more challenging route that takes in the historic city of Cirencester and some of the surrounding countryside. There are some steep hills on this route, so it's best for experienced cyclists.

If you're looking for a more leisurely cycling experience, there are also plenty of shorter routes that can be enjoyed around the Cotswolds. Many of these routes are sign-posted, so it's easy to find your way around.

No matter what your level of experience or fitness, there's a cycling route in the Cotswolds that's perfect for you. So get out there and explore this beautiful part of England on two wheels!

Here are some additional tips for cycling in the Cotswolds:

Wear a helmet and other safety gear.
Be aware of other road users, especially cars and buses.
Obey the speed limit and traffic signs.
Be prepared for all weather conditions.
Carry plenty of water and snacks.
Take breaks often to enjoy the scenery.

With a little planning, you can have a safe and enjoyable cycling experience in the Cotswolds.

2.6 Horseback Riding Adventures

There are many different trails to choose from, ranging from easy rides for beginners to challenging rides for experienced riders.

If you are a beginner, you may want to start with a ride along the River Windrush. This is a flat, easy trail that follows the river through the countryside. You will pass by meadows, forests, and villages along the way.

For a more challenging ride, try the ride up to Broadway Tower. This is a steep climb, but the views from the top are worth it. You can see for miles in every direction.

If you are looking for a more leisurely ride, you can take a ride through the Cotswold Water Park. This is a network of lakes and canals that is perfect for a relaxing ride. You can stop and explore the villages along the way, or just enjoy the peace and quiet of the countryside.

No matter what your level of experience, you are sure to have a great time horseback riding in the Cotswolds. Here are a few of the best places to go:

Cotswold Riding Centre
Bourton-on-the-Water Riding Centre
Cirencester Riding School

If you are looking for a more unique experience, you can try riding a Shire horse. Shire horses are the largest breed of horse in the world, and they are gentle giants. They are perfect for a leisurely ride through the countryside.

No matter where you go or what type of ride you choose, you are sure to have a great time horseback riding in the Cotswolds. The scenery is beautiful, the horses are gentle, and the people are friendly. So saddle up and get ready for an adventure!

Here are some additional tips for planning your horseback riding trip to the Cotswolds:

Book your ride in advance. This is especially important during the peak season (April-September).

Wear comfortable clothing and shoes. You will be doing a lot of walking, so make sure you wear shoes that you can move around in easily.

Bring sunscreen and a hat. The sun can be strong in the Cotswolds, so it is important to protect yourself from the elements.

Bring water and snacks. You will be working up a sweat, so it is important to stay hydrated.

Have fun! Horseback riding is a great way to explore the Cotswolds and enjoy the beautiful countryside.

2.7 Outdoor Activities and Sports

There are plenty of opportunities for hiking, biking, fishing, swimming, and more.

Hiking: The Cotswolds is home to a number of well-maintained hiking trails, ranging from easy walks to challenging hikes. Some popular hiking trails include the Cotswold Way, which is a 100-mile trail that runs from Bath to Chipping Campden, and the Windrush Way, which is a 50-mile trail that runs from Bourton-on-the-Water to Cirencester.

Biking: The Cotswolds is also a great place for biking. There are a number of scenic bike paths that wind through the countryside, and there are also a number of bike hire shops where you can rent bikes. Some popular bike paths include the Cotswold Water Park Cycle Route, which is a 15-mile loop that takes you around the Cotswold Water Park, and the Fosse Way, which is a 100-mile Roman road that runs from Bath to Leicester.

Fishing: The Cotswolds is home to a number of rivers and lakes that are perfect for fishing. There are a number of fishing lakes that are open to the public, and there are also a number of rivers that you can fish with a permit. Some popular fishing spots include the River Windrush, the River Coln, and the River Leach.

Swimming: There are a number of swimming spots in the Cotswolds, including rivers, lakes, and outdoor pools. Some popular swimming spots include the River Windrush, the River Coln, and the Cotswold Water Park.

Other activities: In addition to hiking, biking, fishing, and swimming, there are a number of other activities that you can enjoy in the Cotswolds. These include horse riding, rock climbing, golf, and bird watching.

The Cotswolds is a great place to enjoy the outdoors. There are plenty of activities to choose from, and the scenery is beautiful. So what are you waiting for? Come and explore the Cotswolds today!

Here are some additional tips for planning your outdoor adventure in the Cotswolds:

The best time to visit the Cotswolds for outdoor activities is during the spring and summer months (April-September). The weather is usually mild and sunny during these months, and there are plenty of daylight hours to enjoy your activities.

Make sure to dress comfortably and in seasonally appropriate clothing. Additionally, you might want to bring sunglasses, a hat, and sunscreen.

There might not be many places to eat along the journey, so bring snacks or lunch. Possibly carry water bottles as well.

To keep safe, pay attention to your surroundings and take precautions. This include keeping an eye out for oncoming traffic, wildlife, and other dangers.

Enjoy your vacation in the Cotswolds and have fun!

Chapter 3: Historical and Cultural Treasures in the Cotswolds

3.1 Cotswolds' Historic Market Towns

These towns were once important centers of trade and commerce, and they still retain much of their medieval charm.

Here are some of the most popular Cotswolds market towns:

Burford: Burford is one of the most picturesque towns in the Cotswolds. It is located on the River Windrush, and its High Street is lined with timber-framed buildings. Burford is also home to a number of historic churches, including St. Mary's Church, which dates back to the 12th century.

Bibury: Bibury is another popular Cotswolds market town. It is known for its beautiful cottages, which are built in the traditional Cotswolds style. Bibury is also home to the Arlington Row, which is a row of cottages that were built in the 14th century.

Chipping Campden: Chipping Campden is a well-preserved market town that is located in the heart of the Cotswolds. It is known for its Georgian architecture, and its High Street is lined with shops, boutiques, and restaurants. Chipping Campden is also home to a number of historic buildings, including the Cotswolds Museum, which tells the story of the region.

Stroud: Stroud is the largest market town in the Cotswolds. It is known for its woollen industry, and it is home to a number of woollen mills and shops. Stroud is also home to a number of museums, including the Stroudwater Museum, which tells the story of the town's woollen industry.

These are just a few of the many Cotswolds market towns that are worth visiting. Each town has its own unique charm and history, and they all offer a glimpse into the region's rich past.

In addition to their historical significance, Cotswolds market towns are also great places to shop, eat, and drink. There are a wide variety of shops in these towns, selling everything from local produce to handmade souvenirs. There are also many restaurants and pubs in Cotswolds market towns, where you can sample the region's famous cuisine.

If you are looking for a charming and historic place to visit, the Cotswolds market towns are a great option. These towns offer a unique glimpse into the region's rich past, and they are also great places to shop, eat, and drink.

3.2 Stately Homes and Castles

These historic properties offer a fascinating glimpse into the region's rich history and culture.

Here are a few of the most popular stately homes and castles in the Cotswolds:

Barrington Court: This Elizabethan manor house is set in beautiful gardens and is home to a collection of furniture, paintings, and other artifacts.

Bowood House: This Palladian mansion was built in the 18th century and is surrounded by landscaped gardens. The house is home to a collection of art, furniture, and porcelain.

Cotswold Farm Park: This working farm is home to a variety of animals, including rare breeds of cattle, sheep, and pigs. Visitors can learn about traditional farming methods and see how animals are cared for.

Longleat: This Elizabethan manor house is home to a safari park, a working farm, and a number of other attractions.

Sudeley Castle: This 15th-century castle is the final resting place of Queen Katherine Parr. The castle is also home to a number of gardens, including a knot garden and a walled garden.

Wilton House: This Palladian mansion is one of the largest and finest stately homes in England. The house is home to a collection of art, furniture, and other artifacts.

In addition to these popular stately homes and castles, there are many other historic properties in the Cotswolds that are worth visiting. These include manor houses, abbeys, and churches. Visitors can also explore the region's many villages and towns, which are full of character and charm.

The Cotswolds is a beautiful and historic region that is home to a wealth of cultural treasures. Visitors can enjoy exploring the region's stately homes and castles, as well as its many other historical and cultural attractions.

3.3 Museums and Art Galleries

The Cotswolds are home to a number of museums and art galleries, which offer a fascinating glimpse into the history and culture of this beautiful region. Here are a few of the best:

The Cotswold Museum in Cirencester tells the story of the region from prehistoric times to the present day. The museum's collection includes archaeological finds, local history exhibits, and a fine art gallery.

The Cheltenham Art Gallery and Museum is a world-renowned art gallery with a collection of over 8,000 works of art, including paintings, sculptures, and decorative arts. The gallery also holds a number of transient shows all year round.

The Broadway Tower Museum tells the story of the tower's history, and it also has exhibits on local geology, wildlife, and folklore.

The Painswick Rococo Library is home to a collection of over 10,000 books, and it is also a popular venue for weddings and events.

The Stroudwater Steam Railway offers a unique way to see the Cotswolds countryside, and it also has a number of museums and attractions along its route.

These are just a few of the many museums and art galleries in the Cotswolds. Whether you're interested in history, art, nature, or simply want to learn more about this beautiful region, you're sure to find something to interest you.

3.4 Churches and Abbeys

The Cotswolds are home to some of the most beautiful and historic churches and abbeys in England. These buildings are a testament to the rich religious history of the region, and they offer a fascinating glimpse into the lives of people who lived here centuries ago.

Cirencester Abbey is one of the most well-known churches in the Cotswolds. This majestic monastery was once one of England's most significant ecclesiastical institutions and was built in the seventh century. Henry VIII disbanded the abbey in the 16th century, but it was later rebuilt and is now a well-liked tourist attraction.

Another stunning church in the Cotswolds is St. Mary's Church in Bibury. This church was built in the 12th century, and it is famous for its beautiful stained glass windows and its intricate carvings. St.

Mary's Church is a UNESCO World Heritage Site, and it is one of the most photographed churches in England.

If you are interested in learning more about the religious history of the Cotswolds, I recommend visiting one of the many churches or abbeys in the region. These buildings are a fascinating reminder of the rich history of this beautiful part of England.

Here are some of the other churches and abbeys that you can visit in the Cotswolds:

Aylesbury Abbey
Bourton-on-the-Water Parish Church
Chipping Campden Parish Church
Fairford Parish Church
Gloucester Cathedral
Northleach Parish Church
Stow-on-the-Wold Parish Church
Winchcomb Abbey

These are just a few of the many churches and abbeys that you can visit in the Cotswolds. I encourage you to explore the region and discover the many hidden gems that it has to offer.

3.5 Local Festivals and Events

There are many festivals and events held throughout the year that celebrate the area's rich culture and heritage. Here are a few of the most popular events:

Cheltenham Music Festival: This world-renowned classical music festival takes place every year in July. The festival features a wide range of performers, from world-renowned orchestras and soloists to up-and-coming talent.

Cotswold Olimpick Games: This annual event is a celebration of traditional Cotswold sports and games, such as long jump, archery, and wrestling. The games are held in Chipping Campden, and they attract visitors from all over the world.

Blenheim Palace Flower Show: This prestigious flower show is held every year in July at Blenheim

Palace. The show features stunning displays of flowers, plants, and garden design.

Longborough Festival Opera: This summer opera festival is held in Longborough, a village near Cirencester. The festival features a variety of operas, from classic works to new productions.

Chipping Campden Literature Festival: This annual festival features a wide range of authors, poets, and speakers. The festival is held in Chipping Campden, and it attracts visitors from all over the world.

In addition to these major festivals, there are many other events held throughout the year in the Cotswolds. These events celebrate everything from food and drink to history and culture. Here are a few examples:

Bibury Duck Race: This annual event is held on Boxing Day in Bibury. The race features hundreds of ducks racing down the River Coln.

Tetbury Woolsack Races: This annual event is held on the first Saturday in May in Tetbury. The race features men carrying woolsacks on their backs as they race through the town.

Winchcombe Cotswolds Walking Festival: This annual festival takes place in May and June. The festival features a variety of walks, from easy rambles to challenging hikes.

Sensing Nature Guided Walks: These guided walks are held throughout the year in the Cotswolds. The walks are led by experienced guides who help participants to connect with nature.

These are just a few of the many festivals and events that are held in the Cotswolds throughout the year. There is something for everyone, so be sure to check out the local listings when you are planning your visit.

3.6 Traditional Cotswolds Cuisine

The food in the Cotswolds is just as delicious as the scenery, with a focus on fresh, local ingredients.

Here are some of the most popular traditional Cotswolds dishes:

Cotswold lamb: Lamb is a staple of Cotswolds cuisine, and it is often roasted or grilled. The lamb in the Cotswolds is known for its succulent flavor, thanks to the region's rich pastures.

Cotswold ham: Cotswold ham is a type of dry-cured ham that is made from pork from pigs that have been raised in the Cotswolds. The ham is typically cured for several weeks, and it has a rich, smoky flavor.

Cotswold cheese: Cotswold cheese is a type of cheddar cheese that is made in the Cotswolds. The cheese is typically mild and creamy, and it is often used in cheeseboards or on sandwiches.

Cotswold apple cake: Cotswold apple cake is a traditional dessert that is made with apples, sugar, and spices. The cake is typically baked in a cast-iron skillet, and it has a golden brown crust and a moist, flavorful center.

In addition to these traditional dishes, there are many other great places to eat in the Cotswolds. You can find everything from fine dining restaurants to casual pubs, and there is something for everyone to enjoy.

If you are looking for a truly authentic Cotswolds dining experience, be sure to visit one of the many country pubs in the region. These pubs often serve traditional Cotswolds dishes, and they are a great place to meet locals and experience the Cotswolds way of life.

Here are a few of the best country pubs in the Cotswolds:

The Slaughters Arms: This pub is located in the village of Slaughter, and it has been serving food and drink since the 17th century. The pub is known for its traditional Cotswolds dishes, such as roast lamb and Cotswold ham.

The Bird in Hand: This pub is located in the village of Bibury, and it is known for its beautiful setting and its delicious food. The pub has a large garden, and it is a great place to enjoy a meal on a sunny day.

The Old Bell Inn: This pub is located in the village of Stow-on-the-Wold, and it is one of the oldest pubs in the Cotswolds. The pub has a warm and inviting atmosphere, and it is a great place to sample traditional Cotswolds cuisine.

I hope this gives you a taste of the delicious food that you can find in the Cotswolds. If you are planning a trip to the Cotswolds, be sure to try some of these traditional dishes. You won't be disappointed!

3.7 Local Arts and Crafts

The area has a long history of craftsmanship, dating back to the Middle Ages when skilled artisans worked in a variety of trades, including woodworking, metalworking, and pottery. In the 19th century, the Arts and Crafts movement began in the Cotswolds, and the region became a center for innovative design and craftsmanship. Today, the Cotswolds is home to a wide range of artists, craftspeople, and designers who work in a variety of media, including textiles, jewelry, ceramics, and furniture.

Woodworking

Woodworking is one of the oldest crafts in the Cotswolds, and the region is home to a number of skilled woodworkers. Traditional Cotswold furniture is made from oak, ash, and elm, and is characterized by its simple lines and rustic charm. Many woodworkers in the Cotswolds also create custom pieces, such as tables, chairs, and beds.

Metalworking

Metalworking is another traditional craft in the Cotswolds. Skilled metalworkers in the region create a variety of objects, including jewelry, sculptures, and tools. Many metalworkers use traditional methods, such as hand forging and casting, to create their work.

Pottery

Pottery is another popular craft in the Cotswolds. The region is home to a number of potteries, where skilled artisans create a variety of ceramics, including tableware, decorative items, and sculptures. Many potters in the Cotswolds use traditional methods, such as hand-building and wheel-throwing, to create their work.

Textiles

Textiles are another important part of the Cotswolds' arts and crafts scene. The region is home to a number of weavers, dyers, and embroiderers who create a variety of textiles, including clothing, home furnishings, and accessories. Many textile artists in the Cotswolds use traditional methods, such as hand-weaving and hand-dyeing, to create their work.

Jewelry

Jewelry is another popular craft in the Cotswolds. The region is home to a number of jewelers who create a variety of jewelry, including necklaces, earrings, and rings. Many jewelers in the Cotswolds use traditional methods, such as hand-casting and hand-setting, to create their work.

Other crafts

In addition to the crafts mentioned above, the Cotswolds is home to a wide range of other artists and craftspeople who work in a variety of media, including glass, leather, and sculpture. The region's arts and crafts scene is thriving, and there are many opportunities to see and purchase local handmade goods.

If you are interested in learning more about the Cotswolds' arts and crafts scene, there are a number of resources available. The Cotswolds Tourism Board has a website with information on local artists and craftspeople, and there are a number of museums and galleries in the region that feature exhibits on local crafts. You can also find local craftspeople at farmers markets and other events throughout the year.

The Cotswolds is a beautiful region with a rich history of craftsmanship. The area's arts and crafts scene is thriving, and there are many opportunities to see and purchase local handmade goods. If you are looking for a unique and memorable souvenir from your trip to the Cotswolds, be sure to check out the work of local artists and craftspeople.

Chapter 4: Must-See Attractions in the Cotswolds

4.1 Blenheim Palace

In the Cotswolds, Blenheim Palace is a must-see sight. It is the only English country home that is not royal or ecclesiastical and is a UNESCO World

Heritage Site. For John Churchill, 1st Duke of Marlborough, it was constructed in the early 18th century by John Vanbrugh and Nicholas Hawksmoor as a tribute to his victory over the French in the Battle of Blenheim in 1704.

The palace is home to a number of important works of art, including paintings by Rubens, Van Dyck, and Canaletto. It also has extensive gardens, including a water garden, a maze, and a sunken garden.

In addition to its historical and architectural significance, Blenheim Palace is also known as the birthplace of Sir Winston Churchill. Churchill was born in the palace in 1874 and lived there for part of his childhood.

Blenheim Palace is a popular tourist destination and can be visited by guided tour or self-guided tour. It is open year-round, but the best time to visit is during the summer when the gardens are in bloom.

Here are some of the things you can do at Blenheim Palace:

 Take a guided tour of the palace and learn about its history and architecture.
 Visit the State Rooms, which are home to a number of important works of art.
 Explore the gardens, including the water garden, the maze, and the sunken garden.
 Visit the Churchill Museum, which tells the story of Sir Winston Churchill's life and career.
 Have a picnic lunch in the palace grounds.
 Take a boat ride on the lake.
 Enjoy a traditional English afternoon tea in the palace cafe.

Blenheim Palace is a beautiful and historic place that is sure to impress visitors of all ages. It is a great place to learn about British history and culture, and to enjoy a day of leisurely exploration.

4.2 Stratford-upon-Avon

Stratford-upon-Avon is a beautiful market town in the Cotswolds, England. It is best known as the birthplace of William Shakespeare, and is home to a number of attractions related to the famous playwright. Some of the most popular attractions in Stratford-upon-Avon include:

Shakespeare's Birthplace: This is the house where Shakespeare was born in 1564. It is now a museum that tells the story of his life and work.

Anne Hathaway's Cottage: This is the house where Shakespeare's wife, Anne Hathaway, grew up. It is now a museum that tells the story of her life.

Holy Trinity Church: This church is where Shakespeare is buried. It is also home to a number of his family's graves.

Royal Shakespeare Company: This theater company is based in Stratford-upon-Avon. It performs a wide variety of plays, including many of Shakespeare's works.

Swan Theatre: This theater is a replica of the original theater that Shakespeare performed in. It is now used for a variety of performances, including Shakespeare's plays.

In addition to these attractions, Stratford-upon-Avon is also a charming town with a number of other things to see and do. There are plenty of shops, restaurants, and pubs to explore, and the town is also home to a number of beautiful gardens and parks.

If you are interested in learning more about William Shakespeare, or if you are simply looking for a charming town to visit, Stratford-upon-Avon is a great option.

Here are some other things you can do in Stratford-upon-Avon:

Take a walk on the river: The River Avon runs through Stratford-upon-Avon, and it is a great place to take a walk or boat ride.

Visit the Shakespeare Birthplace Trust: The Shakespeare Birthplace Trust is a charity that owns and operates a number of Shakespeare-related attractions in Stratford-upon-Avon.

See a play: There are always a number of plays being performed in Stratford-upon-Avon, including many of Shakespeare's works.

Visit the Shakespeare Centre: The Shakespeare Centre is a museum that tells the story of Shakespeare's life and work.

Take a tour: There are a number of tours available in Stratford-upon-Avon, including walking tours, bus tours, and boat tours.

Here are some tips for planning your trip to Stratford-upon-Avon:

The best time to visit Stratford-upon-Avon is during the spring or fall, when the weather is mild and there are fewer crowds.

Stratford-upon-Avon is a popular tourist destination, so it is a good idea to book your accommodations in advance.

There are a number of different ways to get to Stratford-upon-Avon, including by car, train, or bus.

The town center is walkable, but there are also a number of buses and taxis available.

Stratford-upon-Avon is a great place to visit for a weekend getaway or a longer vacation.

4.3 Gloucester Cathedral

Gloucester Cathedral is a must-see attraction in the Cotswolds. It is a beautiful and historic building that has been standing for over 1,000 years. The cathedral is home to many interesting features, including the tomb of King Edward II, the magnificent stained glass windows, and the intricate carvings.

The cathedral is located in the heart of Gloucester, a charming city in the Cotswolds. The city is easy to reach by train or car, and there is plenty of parking available near the cathedral.

There are a number of things to do at Gloucester Cathedral. You can take a tour of the building, admire the architecture, and learn about the history of the cathedral. You can also attend a service or concert at the cathedral.

Gloucester Cathedral is a popular tourist destination, so it is advisable to book your tickets in advance. You can book tickets online or by calling the cathedral office.

Here are some of the things you can do at Gloucester Cathedral:

Take a tour of the cathedral: The cathedral offers a variety of tours, including a general tour, a tour of the cloisters, and a tour of the tower.

Admire the architecture: The cathedral is a beautiful example of Gothic architecture. The intricate carvings and the stained glass windows are particularly impressive.

Learn about the history of the cathedral: The cathedral has a long and fascinating history. You can learn about the history of the cathedral on a tour or by reading the information boards located throughout the building.

Attend a service or concert: The cathedral hosts a variety of services and concerts throughout the year. You can check the cathedral website for a schedule of upcoming events.

Gloucester Cathedral is a beautiful and historic building that is well worth a visit. If you are planning a trip to the Cotswolds, be sure to add Gloucester Cathedral to your itinerary.

4.4 Warwick Castle

Warwick Castle is a must-see attraction in the Cotswolds. It is a medieval castle that has been in continuous occupation since 1068. The castle is set in beautiful grounds and offers stunning views of the surrounding countryside. Visitors can explore the castle's many towers and turrets, learn about its history, and see its collection of armor and weapons. There are also jousting tournaments, falconry displays, and other events held at the castle throughout the year.

Here are some of the things you can do at Warwick Castle:

Explore the castle's medieval buildings, including the Great Hall, the State Rooms, and the Dungeon.
Learn about the castle's history with interactive exhibits and demonstrations.
See the castle's collection of armor and weapons.
Watch jousting tournaments, falconry displays, and other events.
Enjoy a meal in the castle's restaurant or take a picnic to enjoy in the grounds.

Warwick Castle is a great place to visit for a day out with the family or a romantic weekend getaway. It is a fascinating place to learn about history and enjoy some medieval fun.

Here are some tips for visiting Warwick Castle:

Buy your tickets in advance to avoid long queues.
Arrive early to get the most out of your visit.

Wear comfortable shoes as you will be doing a lot of walking.

Bring a camera to capture your memories.

Allow plenty of time to explore the castle and grounds.

If you are visiting with children, be sure to check out the castle's special events and activities.

4.5 Sudeley Castle and Gardens

Sudeley Castle and Gardens is a beautiful and historic site located in the heart of the Cotswolds. The castle was built in the 15th century and has been home to many famous people over the years, including King Henry VIII's last wife, Catherine Parr. The gardens are stunning and offer stunning views of the surrounding countryside.

Here are some of the things you can do at Sudeley Castle and Gardens:

Explore the castle: The castle is open to the public and you can explore the many rooms and see the exhibits.

Visit the gardens: The gardens are beautiful and offer stunning views of the surrounding countryside. You can walk through the gardens, relax in the Japanese Garden, or take a boat ride on the lake.

See the tombs: Sudeley Castle is the final resting place of Catherine Parr and her daughter, Mary Seymour. You can see their tombs in the church.

Take a tour: There are a number of tours available, including guided tours of the castle and gardens, as well as ghost tours.

Have a picnic: There are a number of picnic areas in the grounds where you can enjoy a meal al fresco.

Enjoy the events: Sudeley Castle hosts a number of events throughout the year, including concerts, festivals, and historical reenactments.

Sudeley Castle and Gardens is a great place to visit for a day out. It is a beautiful and historic site with something to offer everyone.

4.6 Cotswold Wildlife Park and Gardens

Cotswold Wildlife Park and Gardens is a must-see attraction in the Cotswolds. The park is home to over 260 different species of animals, including giraffes, lions, penguins, and meerkats. The park is set in 160 acres of beautiful parkland and gardens, and there is something for everyone to enjoy.

Here are some of the things you can do at Cotswold Wildlife Park and Gardens:

See the animals up close. The park has a variety of exhibits that allow you to get up close to the animals, including the Giraffe Walkway, the Tiger Trail, and the Penguin Beach.

Take a ride on the safari train. The safari train takes you around the park, giving you a chance to see all of the animals in their natural habitats.

Visit the Walled Garden. The Walled Garden is a beautiful oasis in the middle of the park. It is home to a variety of flowers, plants, and trees.

Enjoy a picnic lunch. There are several picnic areas in the park where you can enjoy a leisurely lunch.

Take part in a keeper talk. The park offers a variety of keeper talks throughout the day. These talks are a great way to learn more about the animals and their care.

Meet the animals. The park offers a variety of animal encounters, where you can meet and interact with the animals.

Cotswold Wildlife Park and Gardens is a great place to spend a day with family and friends. It is a fun and educational experience that you will never forget.

Here are some tips for visiting Cotswold Wildlife Park and Gardens:

The park is open all year round, but the best time to visit is during the spring or summer when the weather is warm and sunny.

The park is open from 10am to 6pm, but it is best to arrive early to avoid the crowds.

There is a cafe in the park, but it is advisable to bring your own food and drinks.

The park is wheelchair accessible, but there are some areas that are not suitable for pushchairs.

The park is a popular tourist destination, so it is advisable to book your tickets in advance.

Enjoy your visit to Cotswold Wildlife Park and Gardens!

4.7 Westonbirt Arboretum

Westonbirt Arboretum is a must-see attraction in the Cotswolds. It is home to over 15,000 trees from all over the world, and is a beautiful place to spend a day exploring. The arboretum is divided into three main areas: the Silk Wood, the Downs, and the Old Arboretum.

The Silk Wood is a dog-friendly area of the arboretum, and is a great place to see some of the oldest and most unusual trees in the collection. The Downs is a more open area of the arboretum, and is a great place to enjoy the views of the surrounding countryside. The Old Arboretum is home to some of the most important trees in the collection, and is a great place to learn about the history of the arboretum.

In addition to the trees, Westonbirt Arboretum also has a number of other attractions, including a visitor center, a shop, a restaurant, and a playground. The visitor center has exhibits on the history of the arboretum, and the shop sells a variety of souvenirs and gifts. The restaurant offers a variety of food and drinks, and the playground is a great place for children to let off some steam.

Westonbirt Arboretum is open all year round, and admission is charged. However, there are a number of free events held throughout the year, including music concerts, theater productions, and family events.

Here are some of the things you can do at Westonbirt Arboretum:

Explore the tree collection: There are over 15,000 trees from all over the world at Westonbirt Arboretum, so you're sure to find something you're interested in.

Take a walk or hike: There are miles of paths to explore at Westonbirt Arboretum, so you can find a route to suit your fitness level.

Visit the visitor center: The visitor center has exhibits on the history of the arboretum, as well as a shop and a restaurant.

Attend an event: Westonbirt Arboretum hosts a variety of events throughout the year, including music concerts, theater productions, and family events.

If you're looking for a beautiful and interesting place to visit in the Cotswolds, Westonbirt Arboretum is a great option. With its wide variety of trees, its stunning scenery, and its many attractions, Westonbirt Arboretum is sure to have something to interest everyone.

4.8 Cirencester Park

In the English Cotswolds, on a lovely 1,000 ha (2,500 acres), there is a park called Cirencester Park. The first Earl Bathurst originally planned it as a deer park in the 1700s. Fallow deer and a variety of other animals, including as rabbits, foxes, and badgers, can be seen in the park.

Cirencester Park is a popular spot for walking, running, and cycling. There are also several trails that lead to the top of the nearby hills, which offer stunning views of the surrounding countryside. The park is also home to a number of historical features, including a 17th-century forecourt with yew hedges, and an adjacent garden.

Cirencester Park is a fantastic choice if you're searching for a serene and beautiful location to unwind and take in the splendor of the Cotswolds. The park is free to enter and is open to the public all year round.

Here are some of the things you can do at Cirencester Park:

Take a walk or run on one of the park's many trails.
Ride your bike through the park.
Visit the 17th-century forecourt with yew hedges.
Explore the adjacent garden.
Look for wildlife, such as deer, rabbits, foxes, and badgers.
Enjoy the stunning views of the surrounding countryside from the top of the nearby hills.

Here are some tips for visiting Cirencester Park:

The park is open year-round, but the best time to visit is during the spring or fall when the weather is mild and the flowers are in bloom.
Admission to the park is free.
There are no food or drink concessions within the park, so be sure to bring your own snacks and drinks.
There is a car park located at the entrance to the park.
The park is wheelchair accessible.

Cirencester Park is a beautiful and tranquil place to spend a day exploring the Cotswolds. With its stunning scenery, historical features, and abundance of wildlife, Cirencester Park is a must-see for any visitor to the Cotswolds.

Chapter 5: Insider Tips and Hidden Gems in the Cotswolds

5.1 Off-the-Beaten-Path Villages

Bibury: This tiny village is known for its honey-colored cottages and its idyllic riverside setting. It's a great place to relax and enjoy the peace and quiet.

Lower Slaughter: This village is even smaller than Bibury, but it's just as charming. The main street is lined with shops and cafes, and there's a beautiful village green where you can people-watch.

Upper Slaughter: This village is located just up the road from Lower Slaughter, and it's worth a visit for its stunning views of the surrounding countryside.

Snowshill: This village is home to Snowshill Manor, a quirky museum that houses a collection of eclectic objects collected by the eccentric Charles Paget Wade.

Painswick: This village is known for its "pepperpot" style of architecture, which features distinctive domed roofs. It's also home to Painswick Rococo Garden, a beautiful garden with a unique design.

Winchcombe: This town is located in the heart of the Cotswolds, and it's a great place to explore the local history. The town is home to a number of museums, including the Winchcombe Museum, which tells the story of the town from its Roman origins to the present day.

5.2 Secret Gardens and Parks

Here are some of the best secret gardens and parks in the Cotswolds:

Asthall Manor is a hidden gem located near Burford. The garden is full of beautiful flowers, trees, and shrubs. It is also home to a number of sculptures, including a large bronze statue of a lion.

Sezincote is a Persian-inspired garden located near Chipping Campden. The garden is full of exotic plants and flowers, including a number of rare and unusual species.

Abbotswood is a large garden located near Stow-on-the-Wold. The garden is home to a wide variety of plants, including rhododendrons, azaleas, and camellias. It also has a number of interesting features, such as a Japanese garden and a sunken garden.

Stowell Park is a Georgian manor house with beautiful gardens. The gardens are full of formal lawns, flowerbeds, and trees. They also have a number of interesting features, such as a maze and a grotto.

Hidcote Manor is a Arts and Crafts garden located near Chipping Campden. The garden is full of beautiful flowers, trees, and shrubs. It is also home to a number of unusual features, such as a dovecote and a sundial.

Cotswold Garden Show is a garden festival held every year in July. The festival features a wide variety of gardens, including private gardens, public gardens, and show gardens.

5.3 Local Markets and Shops

There are many great local markets and shops in the Cotswolds, where you can find everything from fresh produce to handmade crafts. Here are a few of my favorites:

Shambles Market in Stroud is a great place to find vintage items, antiques, and locally-made arts and crafts. It's held every Friday and Saturday throughout the year.

Cirencester Markets are held on Friday and Saturday mornings. You'll find fresh produce, meats, cheeses, and other local foods, as well as a variety of other goods.

The Corn Hall Indoor Market in Cirencester is a great place to find fresh produce, meats, cheeses, and other local foods, as well as a variety of other goods. It's open seven days a week.

Moreton-in-Marsh Market is an arts, crafts, and farmers' market that's held every Tuesday. You'll find fresh produce, meats, cheeses, and other local foods, as well as a variety of handmade crafts.

Cheltenham Craft Market is held on the third Saturday of the month on the Promenade. You'll find a variety of handmade crafts, including jewelry, pottery, and paintings.

In addition to these markets, there are many great shops in the Cotswolds that sell everything from clothes and shoes to home goods and souvenirs. Here are a few of my favorites:

The Cotswold Company is a great place to find locally-made gifts and souvenirs. They have a wide selection of items, including pottery, jewelry, and clothing.

The Country Shop is another great place to find locally-made gifts and souvenirs. They have a wide selection of items, including jams, jellies, and other food products.

The Cotswold Bookshop is a great place to find books about the Cotswolds and other local topics. They also have a large selection of fiction and non-fiction books.

The Cotswold Perfumery is a great place to find handmade perfumes and other fragrances. They have a wide selection of scents, and you can even create your own custom perfume.

No matter what you're looking for, you're sure to find it at one of the many great markets and shops in the Cotswolds. So be sure to set aside some time to explore and do some shopping during your visit.

5.4 Quaint Pubs and Tearooms

The Cotswolds is awash with charming pubs and tearooms, perfect for a relaxing break or a hearty meal. Here are a few of my favorites:

The Porch House: This historic inn is one of the oldest in England, dating back to 947 AD. It's now a chic boutique B&B, but it still has a traditional pub on the ground floor. The Porch House is a great place to enjoy a pint of real ale and some classic pub grub, such as fish and chips or a ploughman's lunch.

The Slaughters Country Inn: This welcoming inn is set in beautiful gardens, just a short walk from the town of Cheltenham. The Slaughters has a wide range of beers on tap, as well as a menu of modern British cuisine. In the summer, you can enjoy your meal in the garden, surrounded by flowers and wildlife.

The Royal Oak Tetbury: This traditional Cotswold pub is a great place to sample some of the local produce. The menu features game, fish, and meat dishes, all cooked to perfection. The Royal Oak also has a wide selection of ales and ciders on tap.

The Bell Inn: This 16th-century inn is a popular spot for both locals and visitors. The Bell has a warm and inviting atmosphere, and the food is excellent. The menu features classic dishes such as steak and kidney pie and fish and chips.

The Old Mill Tea Room: This charming tearoom is housed in a converted watermill. The Old Mill offers a variety of teas, cakes, and pastries, as well as light lunches. It's a great place to relax and enjoy the views of the surrounding countryside.

The Cotswold Tea Party: This popular tearoom is known for its traditional English afternoon tea. The Cotswold Tea Party offers a variety of teas, finger sandwiches, scones, and cakes. It's a great place to experience a taste of British culture.

These are just a few of the many great pubs and tearooms in the Cotswolds. With so many options to choose from, you're sure to find the perfect place to relax and enjoy a delicious meal or a refreshing drink.

5.5 Unique Experiences in the Cotswolds

Here are some unique experiences you can have in the Cotswolds:

Hot air balloon ride: Take to the skies and see the Cotswolds from a bird's eye view. This is a truly unforgettable experience, and it's a great way to see the stunning scenery of the Cotswolds.

Lavender farm: The Cotswolds is home to several lavender farms, and they're a great place to go for a relaxing day out. You can take a walk through the fields, pick your own lavender, and learn about the plant. Lavender is a beautiful flower, and it's a great way to experience the Cotswolds in the summer.

Hiking: The Cotswolds is a great place for hiking, and there are trails to suit all levels of experience. Some popular hiking spots include the Cotswold Way, the Painswick Beacon, and the Cleeve Hill. Hiking is a great way to explore the Cotswolds and get some exercise at the same time.

Cotswold village: The Cotswolds is home to many charming villages, each with its own unique character. Some popular villages include Bourton-on-the-Water, Bibury, and Cirencester. Visiting a Cotswold village is a great way to experience the Cotswolds' unique charm and history.

Cheese tasting tour: The Cotswolds is home to some of the best cheese in the UK, and there are several companies that offer cheese tasting tours. You'll get to sample a variety of cheeses, learn about the cheesemaking process, and meet the cheesemakers. Cheese tasting is a great way to learn about the different types of cheese and how they're made.

Gin tasting tour: The Cotswolds is also home to a number of gin distilleries, and there are several companies that offer gin tasting tours. You'll get to sample a variety of gins, learn about the gin-making process, and meet the distillers. Gin tasting is a great way to learn about the different types of gin and how they're made.

Horse-drawn carriage ride: Take a step back in time and experience the Cotswolds in the way that people did centuries ago. There are several companies that offer horse-drawn carriage rides, and it's a great way to see the countryside and explore the villages. Horse-drawn carriage rides are a great way to relax and enjoy the scenery of the Cotswolds.

Wildlife safari: The Cotswolds is home to a variety of wildlife, and there are several companies that offer wildlife safaris. You'll get to see deer, badgers, foxes, and other animals in their natural habitat. Wildlife safaris are a great way to learn about the different types of wildlife that live in the Cotswolds.

Stargazing: The Cotswolds is a great place to go stargazing, as there is very little light pollution. There are several companies that offer stargazing tours, and you'll get to see the Milky Way, constellations, and planets. Stargazing is a great way to experience the beauty of the night sky.

Chapter 6: Practical Information

6.1 Currency and Banking

The currency in the Cotswolds is the British pound (GBP). The exchange rate for the pound is constantly fluctuating, but as of March 2023, it is approximately £1 = $1.30 USD.

Most businesses in the Cotswolds accept credit cards, but it is always a good idea to have some cash on hand, especially for smaller shops and restaurants. There are ATMs located throughout the region, but they may charge a fee for withdrawals.

If you are traveling from outside of the UK, you may want to consider exchanging your currency for pounds before you arrive. You can do this at your local bank or at a currency exchange bureau. Be sure to compare exchange rates before you make a purchase.

Here are some of the banks with branches in the Cotswolds:

Barclays
HSBC
Lloyds Bank
NatWest
Santander

If you need to access your money from an ATM, there are many machines located throughout the Cotswolds. However, be aware that some ATMs may charge a fee for withdrawals.

Here are some of the ATM networks in the Cotswolds:

Link
Cirrus
Plus

If you are traveling with a debit card, be sure to check with your bank to see if there are any fees associated with using it abroad. Some banks charge a foreign transaction fee, which is a percentage of the transaction amount. Others may charge a daily currency conversion fee.

It is also a good idea to let your bank know that you will be traveling abroad. This will help to prevent your card from being blocked if it is used outside of your home country.

Here are some tips for using your credit or debit card in the Cotswolds:

Be sure to keep your PIN number confidential.
Only use your card in secure locations.
Inspect your receipt carefully for any errors.
Report any lost or stolen cards to your bank immediately.

By following these tips, you can help to protect yourself from fraud and ensure that you have a safe and enjoyable trip to the Cotswolds.

6.2 Language and Communication

There are some local dialects that may be unfamiliar to visitors. For example, the word "daps" is used in some parts of the Cotswolds to refer to shoes, and the word "scant" is used to mean "small" or "insufficient."

If you are not familiar with the local dialect, it is always best to ask for clarification if you are unsure of what someone is saying. You can also try to learn a few basic phrases in the local dialect before you visit. This will help you to communicate more effectively with the locals and make your trip more enjoyable.

Here are a few basic phrases in the Cotswold dialect:

"How are you?" = "Ow bist?"
"I'm fine, thanks." = "Oi be fairish, thanks."
"Where are you from?" = "Wheer be ee from?"

"I'm from (your hometown)." = "Oi be from (your hometown)."
"It's nice to meet you." = "It be nice ta meet thee."
"Goodbye." = "Ta-ra."

You can also find a more comprehensive list of Cotswold dialect phrases online.

In addition to English, there are a number of other languages spoken in the Cotswolds. The most common of these are French, German, and Spanish. If you are fluent in one of these languages, you may be able to use it to communicate with locals. However, it is important to note that English is the primary language of the Cotswolds, and you may have difficulty finding someone who speaks your language fluently.

If you need to communicate with someone who does not speak English, you can try using a translator. There are a number of free online translators available, and you can also find translators in most major tourist destinations.

Here are a few websites that offer free online translation services:

Google Translate: https://translate.google.com/
Bing Translate: https://www.bing.com/translator/
DeepL Translate: https://www.deepl.com/translator

If you are planning to travel to the Cotswolds, it is a good idea to learn a few basic phrases in the local dialect. This will help you to communicate more effectively with the locals and make your trip more enjoyable. You can also find a number of free online translation services that can be helpful if you need to communicate with someone who does not speak English.

6.3 Safety and Health

The Cotswolds is a very safe region for tourists and locals alike. It is known for its beautiful rural scenery and friendly people. However, there are a few safety and health tips that visitors should keep in mind while traveling in the area.

Driving: The most important safety tip is to remember to drive on the left side of the road. This may take some getting used to, especially for visitors from countries where they drive on the right. Be sure to be aware of your surroundings and drive slowly, especially in rural areas where there may be livestock or other unexpected obstacles on the road.

Walking and Hiking: The Cotswolds is a great place to go for walks and hikes. However, it is important to be aware of the weather conditions and to dress appropriately. Be sure to wear sturdy shoes or boots, and bring plenty of water and snacks. If you are planning on hiking in remote areas, it is a good idea to let someone know where you are going and when you expect to be back.

Biking: Biking is another great way to explore the Cotswolds. However, it is important to be aware of the traffic and to ride defensively. Be sure to wear a helmet and bright clothing, and obey all traffic laws.

Water Sports: The Cotswolds is home to a number of rivers and lakes, which are popular for swimming, canoeing, and kayaking. However, it is important to be aware of the water conditions and to swim only in designated areas. Be sure to wear a life jacket if you are planning on participating in any water sports.

Wildlife: The Cotswolds is home to a variety of wildlife, including deer, foxes, and badgers. It is important to be aware of the wildlife and to take precautions to avoid any encounters. Do not feed the animals, and keep your distance if you see any wildlife.

By following these safety tips, you can help to ensure a safe and enjoyable trip to the Cotswolds.

Here are some additional safety and health tips for travelers to the Cotswolds:

Be aware of the weather conditions: The weather in the Cotswolds can change quickly, so it is important to be prepared for all types of weather. Be sure to pack a raincoat, sunscreen, and a hat.

Stay hydrated: The Cotswolds can be a very dry region, so it is important to drink plenty of water.

Eat healthy foods: The Cotswolds is home to a number of great restaurants, but it is also a good idea to pack some healthy snacks for your trip.

Get enough sleep: Getting enough sleep will help you to stay healthy and energized while you are traveling.

Take breaks: Don't try to do too much on your trip. Take some time to relax and enjoy the scenery.

By following these safety and health tips, you can help to ensure a safe and enjoyable trip to the Cotswolds.

6.4 Useful Contacts

Here are some useful contacts in the Cotswolds:

Tourist Information Centres
   Cirencester Tourist Information Centre: 01285 655555
   Cheltenham Tourist Information Centre: 01242 237237

Stow-on-the-Wold Tourist Information Centre: 01451 830333

Police

Gloucestershire Constabulary: 101

Fire Service

Gloucestershire Fire and Rescue Service: 999

Ambulance Service

South Western Ambulance Service: 999

Hospitals

Gloucestershire Royal Hospital: 01452 311111

Cheltenham General Hospital: 01242 223333

Doctors

There are many doctors' surgeries in the Cotswolds. You can find a list of surgeries in your area by visiting the NHS website.

Pharmacies

There are also many pharmacies in the Cotswolds. You can find a list of pharmacies in your area by visiting the NHS website.

Public Transport

The Cotswolds are well served by public transport. There are buses and trains that can take you to most places in the region. You can find more information about public transport in the Cotswolds by visiting the Traveline website.

Car Rental

If you are planning on driving in the Cotswolds, you will need to hire a car. There are many car rental companies located in the region. You can find more information about car rental in the Cotswolds by visiting the RAC website.

Accommodation

There are many hotels, B&Bs, and guesthouses in the Cotswolds. You can find more information about accommodation in the Cotswolds by visiting the Visit Cotswolds website.

6.5 Internet and Connectivity

The Cotswolds is a rural area, so internet access is not as widespread or as fast as it is in urban areas. However, there are a number of options available for those who need to stay connected.

Broadband

Broadband is the most common type of internet connection in the Cotswolds. It is available in most areas, but speeds can vary depending on your location. If you are planning to work from home or stream movies online, you will need to make sure that you have a fast enough connection.

Mobile Broadband

Mobile broadband is another option for staying connected in the Cotswolds. It is available in all areas, but speeds can be slower than broadband. Mobile broadband is a good option for those who need to be able to work or access the internet on the go.

Wi-Fi

Wi-Fi is available in many public places in the Cotswolds, such as cafes, libraries, and hotels. This can be a convenient way to stay connected if you only need to use the internet for a short period of time.

Public Wi-Fi Safety

When using public Wi-Fi, it is important to be aware of the security risks. Public Wi-Fi networks are not always secure, so it is important to take precautions to protect your personal information. You should avoid using public Wi-Fi for sensitive activities, such as online banking or credit card transactions. You should also use a strong password and enable a firewall on your device.

Coworking Spaces

If you are looking for a place to work that has fast internet access and a professional environment, consider checking out a coworking space. Coworking spaces are becoming increasingly popular in the Cotswolds, and they offer a variety of amenities, such as meeting rooms, printers, and coffee.

Internet Cafes

If you are looking for a more affordable option for internet access, consider checking out an internet cafe. Internet cafes are typically located in urban areas, and they offer basic internet access for a fee.

There are a number of options available for staying connected in the Cotswolds. The best option for you will depend on your needs and budget. If you need a fast and reliable connection, broadband is the best option. If you are on a budget or only need to use the internet for a short period of time, mobile broadband or public Wi-Fi may be a better option.

6.6 Packing Essentials

1. Comfortable walking shoes or boots: You'll be doing a lot of walking, so make sure your shoes are comfortable and supportive.

2. Waterproof jacket: The weather in the Cotswolds can be unpredictable, so it's always a good idea to pack a waterproof jacket.

3. Rain pants: If you're planning on doing any hiking, rain pants are a must-have.

4. Hat and gloves: The weather in the Cotswolds can be cold in the winter, so pack a hat and gloves.

5. Sunglasses: The sun can be strong in the Cotswolds, so pack a pair of sunglasses.

6. Sunscreen: The sun can be strong in the Cotswolds, so pack sunscreen.

7. Insect repellent: There can be insects in the Cotswolds, so pack insect repellent.

8. Camera: The Cotswolds is a beautiful place, so you'll want to bring your camera to capture the memories.

9. Portable charger: If you're planning on doing a lot of exploring, you'll need a way to keep your devices charged.

10. Day bag: You'll need a day bag to carry your essentials with you when you're exploring.

11. Travel towel: A travel towel is small and lightweight, making it perfect for packing.

12. Water bottle: Stay hydrated by packing a reusable water bottle.

13. Snacks: Pack some snacks to keep you energized throughout the day.

14. Book: Bring a book to read on the beach or in your hotel room.

15. Playing cards: Playing cards are a great way to pass the time on a rainy day.

16. Journal: Keep a journal to record your memories of your trip.

17. Camera tripod: If you're serious about photography, a camera tripod can help you take sharper photos.

18. Hiking poles: If you're planning on doing any serious hiking, hiking poles can help you save energy and prevent injuries.

19. First-aid kit: A first-aid kit is always a good idea to have on hand, just in case.

20. Map: A map can help you get around and find your way back to your hotel.

6.7 Etiquette and Cultural Norms

The Cotswolds is a rural area in England, and as such, it has its own unique set of etiquette and cultural norms. Here are a few things to keep in mind when visiting the Cotswolds:

Be respectful of the countryside. The Cotswolds is a beautiful area, and it's important to respect the natural environment. This means disposing of trash properly, not littering, and respecting wildlife.

Be aware of your surroundings. The Cotswolds is a popular tourist destination, so it's important to be aware of your surroundings and be mindful of other people. This means being considerate of noise levels, not blocking pathways, and giving way to oncoming traffic.

Dress appropriately. The Cotswolds is a rural area, so it's important to dress appropriately. This means wearing comfortable shoes, layers of clothing, and sunscreen.

Be polite and friendly. The people of the Cotswolds are known for being friendly and welcoming, so it's important to be polite and friendly when interacting with locals. This means saying hello and goodbye, making eye contact, and being respectful of their customs.

Here are some additional tips for etiquette and cultural norms in the Cotswolds:

When dining out, it is customary to tip your server 10-15% of the bill.
It is not considered polite to talk on your cell phone in public.
When meeting someone for the first time, it is customary to shake hands.
It is considered polite to dress modestly when visiting churches and other religious buildings.
It is not considered polite to smoke in public places.

By following these tips, you can ensure that you have a pleasant and respectful experience while visiting the Cotswolds.

Conclusion

Congratulations! You have reached the end of our "Cotswolds Travel Guide." We hope this comprehensive resource has ignited your wanderlust and provided you with valuable insights to make your Cotswolds adventure truly unforgettable.

As you prepare to embark on your journey, we want to leave you with a few parting thoughts. The Cotswolds is a region that transcends time, captivating visitors with its timeless beauty, rich history, and vibrant culture. It is a place where you can immerse yourself in nature, connect with the friendly locals, and experience the true essence of rural England.

Whether you choose to wander through the postcard-perfect villages, hike along scenic trails, explore historic landmarks, or simply indulge in the region's culinary delights, the Cotswolds offers a multitude of experiences that will leave a lasting impression on your heart and soul.

Remember, in the Cotswolds, every moment is an opportunity for serendipitous discovery. Take the time to meander along hidden footpaths, strike up conversations with locals, and embrace the slower pace of life. Allow yourself to be swept away by the Cotswolds' ineffable charm, as you create memories that will stay with you long after your journey comes to an end.

As you bid farewell to the Cotswolds, we encourage you to carry the spirit of this enchanting region with you. Let it inspire you to seek beauty in the everyday, to find solace in nature, and to appreciate the rich tapestry of cultures that exist around the world.

Remember, the Cotswolds will always welcome you back with open arms. Its timeless allure and indescribable magic will forever hold a special place in your heart. So, until we meet again, may your travels be filled with wonder, adventure, and the joy of discovering new horizons.

Safe travels!

Appendix: Cotswolds Travel Resources

As a bonus, we have included an appendix that provides you with a list of recommended websites and apps to enhance your Cotswolds travel experience. These resources will help you navigate the region, find the best accommodations, discover local events, and uncover hidden gems that may not be mentioned in this guide. Make sure to explore these resources to make the most of your time in the Cotswolds.

- Recommended Websites and Apps

Rick Steves Europe: This website has a wealth of information on the Cotswolds, including articles, travel tips, and itineraries.

The Cotswolds Tourist Board: This official website of the Cotswolds Tourist Board has information on all aspects of visiting the region, including attractions, accommodation, and events.

Cotswolds.com: This website is a great resource for finding things to do in the Cotswolds, including walking and cycling trails, pubs, restaurants, and shops.

Cotswold Way App: This app provides detailed information on the Cotswold Way, a long-distance footpath that runs through the heart of the Cotswolds.

National Trust App: This app provides information on all of the National Trust properties in the Cotswolds, including opening hours, admission prices, and directions.

Google Map: Google Maps is a great resource for planning your trip to the Cotswolds. You can use it to find your way around, find places to stay, and find things to do. You can also use it to create custom maps that will help you plan your itinerary.

Here are some of the things you can do with Google Maps:

Find your way around: Google Maps has detailed maps of the Cotswolds, so you can easily find your way around. You can use the search bar to find specific locations, or you can use the map's navigation features to get directions from one place to another.

Find places to stay: Google Maps has a comprehensive list of hotels, bed and breakfasts, and other accommodations in the Cotswolds. You can use the filters to narrow down your search by price, location, and amenities.

Find things to do: Google Maps has a list of attractions, restaurants, and other activities in the Cotswolds. You can use the filters to narrow down your search by type of activity, location, and price.

Create custom maps: Google Maps allows you to create custom maps that will help you plan your itinerary. You can add markers for places you want to visit, and you can even add notes and photos.

Made in United States
Troutdale, OR
08/03/2023

11754475R00076